Femme
du Monde

Femme du Monde

[WOMAN OF THE WORLD]

POEMS

BY

PATRICIA SPEARS JONES

TIA CHUCHA PRESS
LOS ANGELES

acknowledgments

Thanks to the editors of the following publications in which these poems previously appeared:

Best American Poetry 2000, "Ghosts" ed. by Rita Dove, Scribners, New York, 2000
Blood & Tears: Poems for Matthew Shepard, "My Matthew Shepard Poem", ed. by Scott Gibson, Painted Leaf Press, New York, 1999
Court Green, "Cat on a Hot Tin Roof or Liz in Lingerie"
www.mipoesias, *"How to Marry a Millionaire"*
Barrow Street, "Hope, Arkansas, 1970"
Barrow Street, "La Grand horologe at Musee d Orsay"
Warpland: A Journal of Black Literature and Ideas, "Female Trouble"
Bomb, "Comfort and Joy"
*The Best of Callaloo,*Vol.24, "Shack With Vines"
Heliotrope, "Laura "
The World #56/67, "The Village Sparkles" and *"Hud"*
Agni 49, "Sapphire"
Crab Orchard Review, "Belissima" and "Ghosts"
Barrow Street "Days of Awe" and *"Red River"*
The World #53, "Comme des Garcons"
The Yalobusha Review,"Emergency Eye Wash"
Callaloo, Vol. 19 "Thanksgiving" *"Saltimbanque"* "Shack With Vines" and "All Saints Day"

Note: "Days of Awe" was selected for a letter press broadside from the Center for Book Arts, New York City, February, 2002.

I am deeply grateful to Carrie Mae Weems for the gorgeous photograph that graces the collection's cover. A special thank you goes to Mary Baine Campbell, Peter Covino, Cornelius Eady, Barbara Elovich, Janet Goldner, Scott Hightower, Janet Kaplan, Quraysh Ali Lansana, John Edward McGrath, Linda Raskin, Nathalie Schmidt, and Susan Wheeler for their critical comments and encouragement; and to Joan Simon and her family for their hospitality in Paris and Gregory Pardlo, Jr. for his editorial assistance.

These poems were created with the support of grants from The Goethe Institute (Boston) for travel/research in Germany, The National Endowment for the Arts, The Foundation for Contemporary Art, and the New York Foundation for the Arts; and residencies at The Virginia Center for the Creative Arts and The Millay Colony for the Arts. Thank you.

Book Design: Jane Brunette
Cover Photo: Carrie Mae Weems

PUBLISHED BY:
Tia Chucha Press
A Project of Tia Chucha's Centro Cultural
PO Box 328
San Fernando, CA 91341
www.tiachucha.com

DISTRIBUTED BY:
Northwestern University Press
Chicago Distribution Center
11030 South Langley Avenue
Chicago, IL 60628

Tia Chucha Press is supported by the National Endowment for the Arts and operating funds from Tia Chucha's Centro Cultural. Tia Chucha's Café & Centro Cultural have received support from the Los Angeles Department of Cultural Affairs, the Center for Cultural Innovation, the Middleton Foundation, Not Just Us Foundation, the Liberty Hill Foundation, Youth Can Service, Toyota Sales, Solidago Foundation, and other grants and donors including Bruce Springsteen, John Densmore, Dan Attias, Dave Marsh, Suzan Erem, Cynthia Cuza, Mel Gilman, Tony & Jennie LoRe, Denise Chávez and John Randall of the Border Book Festival, and Luis & Trini Rodríguez.

Contents

ϟ

PART I

ϟ

PART II

꛰

Part III

꛰

Part IV

For Charlotte Carter,

Margo Jefferson,

and

Maureen Owen

Quando si parte il gioco de la zara
colui che perde si riman dolent,
repetendo le volte, e tristo impara;
con l'altro se ne va tutta la gente

When the game of chance breaks up
the loser is left disconsolate
repeating his throws, sadly learning
people hang out with the winner.

Canto VI
Il Purgatorio, The Divine Comedy
(Author's translation)

Part One

Hope, Arkansas 1970

A wealthy white man drives up to the golden arches—Texas plates.
It's a Mercedes sedan, luxuriantly glistening. And from the passenger side,
emerges a blonde child, made up—tarted up, as a Brit would say.

We were freshmen girls on the way to our suite mate's wedding.
Starting out from Memphis, the Mississippi whipping up currents,
we've crossed Arkansas from East to West—Dallas our destination.

We sung silly songs to curb Nancy's fear of crossing bridges to
a smiling hatred of girls singing off-key, raucously. It worked. We're here.
But, who is this man to this child? Father, lover, dirty old uncle.

We put down our milkshakes, sandwiches and fries.
The little blonde chatters away. The man strokes her hand.
The girls we are become womanly, matronly.
We want to rescue this child.

But where would we take her?
And what would happen to all that money?

≫ FOR NANCY HOWELL

hosts

He was filled with beauty, so filled he could not stop the shadows
from their walk around his horn, blasting cobwebs in the Fillmore's ceiling.

Somewhere dawn makes up for the night before, but he is floating.
Dead in the water. And yet, my lover tells me, he saw him shimmering.

As did others. It could have been the acid. Or fragmented harmonics.
His reed ancestral. This perilous knowledge. The band went home,

shivering. A girl threw roses in the water. Carnations, daisies. And bright red sashes.
Like ones the Chinese use for funeral banners. A drummer intoned chants

From the Orient. Police wrote up the news. Years later, my lover told me
Friends would hear the whisper, then a tone, full throttle from the wind.

Ghosts on Second Avenue, jazzmen in the falling stars.
If you catch one, your hands will glitter.

Belissima

What to make of the Zairian's virile smile?
No snake slithers with such style.
No cock crows as loudly and yet
when a whisper is needed,
his breath is as soft as an infant's cooing.

Belissima. Zouk music is as bright as day-
light above white white beaches
Oh yes, this is the way to sway
into the sweet singer's mirth

chorus responds in syncopation
to his commands. We join the harmonies
in words from a language
earthbound and utterly delicate.

As his mouth flames intoxication
Congolese rhythms, homesickness, and beauty's power
to disrupt,
the Chicago girls get wasted, somewhat
in the miracle of shadowed lust.

Zouk music in the snowbelt.
Sex on the beach

❧ FOR DEBORAH

Days of Awe

I feel as if my life were held together by wishful thinking
and krazy glue. Somehow it works.
Somehow all our lives work.
Full moons or Fridays the 13th, mysterious are the ways of the spirit.
Or the ways we dream ourselves awake.

Each morning a cloudless day revels in the impossible,
the dispensation of shadows. It is a ruse. God gives
and God thinks things over. And while the pondering abides,
each of us has time to act one way or the other.
Give, get. Build, destroy. Laugh and laugh some more.

Splendor in the heavens, ashes on earth.
Love conjured, love lost.
Out of the corner of my myopic right eye, I spy
a white van curving towards me, Sebastian at the wheel.
Face unscarred, but that's not the real story.
Out of the Bronx, into the modest comforts of Brooklyn,
he smiles the smile of a man redeemed in blood.

We do not stand still. The last of the roses open petulantly,
daring summer to end. Oh days of uncommon beauty,
when the knotted heart unties itself. As trees old and young
starve their leaves into gold, flame, rust.

➤ FOR CYNTHIA KRAMAN

Comme des Garcons

The Italians really know how to do red,
now it is the Japanese.
Poised on poured concrete, this vivid scarlet
expensively, carefully cut, harlot,
silk as parachute.

A midnight purple velvet brushes the hand
catlike as if in conversation with the silk.
Persian versus Siamese?

A chaste white slithers the length of mannequins
oddly shaped as if female form is an afterthought.

Under the stern lights suave white floats a line
of solitude, crystalline as first snowfall,
forgetful of the swift human charge
that takes to pulling threads from the elaborately
disguised seams, splatters white water,
scars every attempt at human perfection.

Like this green jacket suddenly male.
Will the actor buy it?
Will it work for all the other boys?

Ascending the brutal staircases towards
chaste white and harlot red, lipstick luscious,
what matters if the forms dematerialize leaving sex,
solitude, and the frank shapes of credit for contemplation.

Elsewhere, all is feline.

Part Two

apphire

> ON MY FAVORITE EPISODE OF AMOS N' ANDY, KINGFISH COMES
> HOME WITH FOUND MONEY, LOTS OF IT AND SAYS TO HIS WIFE, SAPPHIRE:
> "I'VE ALWAYS PROMISED TO BRING HOME THE BACON. WELL, HONEY,
> I BROUGHT YOU THE WHOLE HOG."

I swore to a friend that yes, you can live on martinis and chocolate!
Dark chocolate, real chocolate, slightly bitter and lovely to smell.

And it helps to have a working knowledge of languages other than English:
French, perhaps German or Spanish.
This will serve one well from Brussels to Krakow.

Entertain your learned hosts. Toss in expertise, opinion, and artful snobbery.
Baraka and Yeats, poetry, theater, cultural inquiry, any good reason to party.
Well, party on. What a swank notion, the Black sophisticate
with a working knowledge of Celtic mythology and hoodoo, shouts and blues.

Sophisticated lady. Walking this tensile rope that swings between pocketbook
       and fantasy.
This side Paradise. That side bankruptcy.
Who cares if the woods are scary, dark and deep?
German food is gray, white and green, the sausages brown.
Winter food. Winter people.

The *Lenbachhaus* empty but for the curator, an interpreter and me. We walk
       at a pace
known only to museum workers—respectful, professional, with time enough
       for the surprise,
the find, a reverent glance. There is danger here and dedication.

Franz Marc's fantastic horses swirling reds, yellows, an impossible purplish blue.
Read birth dates and death notices. World War I—destroyer of artists.
There is our heroine. The girlfriend or wife who will not sacrifice

one measure of her talent even as her beloved recoils
from his promise of a perfect union made in art.

Left at the train station, in an airport, on the side of the road,
women have always been wise to scrap and savvy composing
canvasses of prodigious color and luminosity. It is not always

night in our soul of souls. Just a weak ache for what could have been.
We were raised to recognize the brute's soft smile and the trickster's violent
        craft, but
not the tender one's evolving desire, his roving eye, his voice crashing against
        our tears.

Who is to blame? The ideal of it all. Gabriele Munter stopped not once the
        making of
her art. How could she, when her lover stopped not the making of his, only
        his love for her.

Blue, blue, blue rider. *Blaue Reiter* see what you have left behind.
Paintings dance and marvel, assume aspects of magic, prophecy, precision
        and dread.
Iron works forged a martial steel. Gunpowder, dynamite, munitions,
        munificence.

And yes, she hid from the Nationalist Socialists remnants of pre-war
        experiments
essaying the values of colors, shapes, the artists' place beneath the dismal
        stars to come.

This is how the story spends itself, late twentieth century on the wide
boulevards of great European cities where the dust and trouble
of war and revival stratify the effortless rebuilding.

A plaque in the plaza marking a speech, a battle, the death of one great man
or a tribe's lonely disaster. Rings of fire or rings of gold.
Sooner or later a story unfolds.

What matters is that I stood there, three days before Palm Sunday, 1989
eyeing the elaborate chocolate rabbits in the window of a Munich confectioner.

The sweet hare's fabled face-whiskers shiver in the icy breeze of air conditioning.
His ears proportioned, listening for our appreciation.

You really want panic? Think of the chocolateer's skill.
How for every perfect bunny in the window,
hundreds lie in pieces awaiting his children's ready mouths.

Ah, the kids get the damaged goods for that is the way of the world.
And they lick the brutalized ears with much joy.

La grande horologe at Musee d'Orsay

I walked the *Quai Voltaire* until I found the plaque on the building
where Nureyev must have seduced who knows how many pretty young men.
In magazines, those rooms wore striped wallpaper
and huge paintings of well-muscled boys.
His bathtub was copper and deep.
A masculine scent drifts from the *Seine*.

Sun filters delicately through the systems of gray that define a Parisian sky.
Sunlight is as dear as the wall coverings, the gilt frames, those rare,
      costly woods
shaping tables, desks, commodes and cushioned chairs; the supple
      leather goods
that take pride of place in the high end shop windows.
A way of the world is for sale and has been for centuries.

A city composed by regal commands; followed by bourgeois' demands—
Elegant architecture at a good price.

Why envy a place where clocks wear crowns?
And good wine can be found in workingmen's cafes?

La grande horologe sits in this wonderful grid
a mass of baroque gestures created for an age
that simultaneously mocked the future
as it mimicked the past.
How else to explain the ornate finish, elaborate curves,
the roman numerals precisely centered in ivory ovals,
how else to follow the lengthy hands
as they travel the circle from midnight to noon
cherishing the traces of time grabbed or time lost

World weary or rank innocents, busy, cheerful, hopeful, anxious,
      in love or lust,

those who once faced this clock's classical numbers are recalled
            in the mass of tourists,
earnestly searching for Van Gogh's disheveled bed
or Manet's treasured dreams— a world of clothed men and naked women.
Each of us romanced by the drama of this space, the clock face stopped.
Time as an architecture of echo. Memory damned.

The guards shoo us away from the marble statues that defined
            the whisper of grief
that was Belle Époque.
And we welcome the diversion.
Someone prepares a perfect crepe, and the colored men and women:
African, Vietnamese, Chinese, Arab pour the coffee,
sweep the floors, dust the gold glaze
and warm the cold marble that erupts in rooms
the size of small suburban homes. When time passes,
it walks like the women in Cocteau films,
haughty, dangerous or innocent of darkness until the darkness comes.

In the room of Van Gogh's paintings,
where the light mapped a longitude of glee,
waves of colors motion the familiar:
a bed, a tree, haystacks, stars.
I stood as if transfixed in an earthquake.
Stopped by the manmade.

Comfort and Joy

The whiteface clown rolls out of clown alley like a whippet at the dog track.
He's stopped in his mad march by the August who makes the most marvelous
of grimaces.
Fascinated, sugar-loaded pink and chubby children squeal like piglets.

Slay me
Slay me
pleads an old man in last year's sports coat.
SLAY ME!

Trained beasts turn their generous bodies, roar, growl moan.
Their human partners step outside, spy the expanding stars,
smoke forbidden cigarettes. Pray.

In center ring, the lead tamer enters the stench and dream
of the lion's cage, flashes even white teeth and a practiced whip.
The big cats lick, roll, and tease.
Where's the blood?

The colorful band pitches a martial melody
as the aerialists ascend to their conjugal dance.

Could they miss the breath that leads to first touch?
Will they find that moment that defies the idea of air?

The audience gasps, applauds as the couple's sequined costumes
fracture light. They descend to the floor, bow deeply, then run—
he to the east; she to the west
as if from the dream of a happy marriage.

The ringmaster tosses his rainbow hat high
extends the crowd a grand farewell.

The audience reluctantly leaves. Astonished by the beasts' blood,
the clowns tiny cars; the smell of pleasure spent. Still.
They stumble into a night illuminated by strands of bright naked bulbs,
electric pendants crossing this field of vision,
casting forth the moon's corrupted globe and
the faintest rays from Venus' distant seductions.

Satisfied in their security, lit by the carnival's utilitarian lights,
the audience navigates invisible paths
to that tribal notion of comfort and joy some call the American Paradise.

➤ IN MEMORY OF FELIX GONZALEZ TORRES

Emergency Eye Wash

Accidents will happen, remember

Was it the price of something or the time needed
to clean out the garage? Was it anything important—
no sex for weeks or an unfamiliar shade
of nail polish streaking an old pair of blue jeans?

Who started the heat in this kitchen?
And why are we waiting for the doctor to emerge?

My eye, you screamed.
My eye!

And off we drove to the hospital. Your hand sheltering
the side of you I still loved.
Your eye drowned in toxins.
Where did they come from?
What had you rubbed?
I hated your being in danger.
The very idea of you half-blind.

The doctor takes you away from me.
A neutralizing agent enters your poisoned eye.
You've been purged. No residual damage. Lucky.

You're so lucky.
You'll stay a few more months.
We will kiss, fight, kiss again.

Then one day you will turn left
when you should have turned right.

Over. Done. A life gone. Twenty five.
Widowed at twenty two. Happy. Me.
But I tell no one.
I just cry.

Shack With Vines

Who lives in this motley house?
Some old woman left back of
the bottom of the county.

She's crazy. No, she's poor.
She makes her taste of something
as bitter as the broad leaves

choking the last of life from her house.

Did she go to church each Sunday?
Pull the yellow streamers during the Maypole dance?
Learn the first four chapters of Genesis
by the age of nine?

Where is her family?
Or was there not a family?
Did she nurse the folk of the county?
Is this the conjure woman, so talked about?

Or is the resident of this dying house male?
Shotgun at his bedside, ready
to blast aside the wicked.

This is his sanctuary, this little house.
Away from the highway,
far outside of town.

Far from the many temptations of the flesh,
about which he reads repeatedly in weak daylight.

Or are there orphaned children sleeping beneath blankets,
coats, whatever warmth was left behind?
They remember electricity, hot showers, macaroni and cheese.

Scavengers in the town, their T-shirts, old jeans,
and itchy, unwashed sweaters contour skinny backs.
There they are outside the local fast food drive-in

sifting through the cast off bread and meat,
laughter tossed over the bin like an acidulent anecdote.

Shack collapsing.

Why I Left the Country: A Suite

THE SUBURBAN DREAM

The house could be anywhere—desert, valley,
mountainside—lucre and luck find the site.

There is much told pleasure culled from the perfected house.
Sniff the floorboards, stroke the gold and brass fixtures, slide fingers
along suave counter tops, behold high ceiling's profligate beams,
drape the snake-coiled cosmology of infrastructure across the architect's
drafting table.

Dream the developer's glossy dream.
Delight in worlds produced with pencils, hammers, paper and glass.

You'd think this wonderful.
You'd be suburban.

A Gallant History

The austerity of luxuriant rural life can be spiteful.
On neighbors' properties, orphaned dogs
and uncompromising cats rant flagrant music
as they plunder garbage and rachet trees.

A full moon limns a vigil for the dream house:
tales of bourbon bottles stashed behind the bronze umbrella stand;
a garden hoe used to discipline an errant servant
who flirtatious said "good morning" to the madam who swooned;
frayed velvet and satin ribbons colored rouge, silver, opal and gold
gird the rotting love letters of long dead maiden aunts;
unbleached yellowed stains on the maid's narrow mattress
the whispered "no" unheard.

Where are the wildflowers and the humdrum magic of tea?

The City Proper

The crosstown bus is due any minute.
Satisfied commuters stoop to lift bags of carefully purchased stuff:
costumes for the latest wave in carnival fetes;
cosmetics for a firmer face and thigh;
jewels for passing about in private.
A lucent fire.

Dinner is picaresque.
A tableaux of gestures in the making of feasts.
Lemongrass, cilantro, hominy, wine.
At midnight, everyone is exhausted in town
and out.

One minute past the witching hour, where is that divine waiter?
He forgot to bring my check.

The Village Sparkles

In German, Vagina is always capitalized.
It is subject, therefore, important.

In America, who knows what is important.
Julia Roberts or Vagina or Julia Roberts and Vagina.

Actually, this is a dodge. My hand hurts.
My heart aches. Intemperate spices breach summer air

and yet, I blush. Nutmeg, cinnamon. Who can handle Spring or
Penis in Winter. Cardamom, ginger. Garlic for Luck.

Who cares about Dream?
Important, subject.

Action. Where is action? If we weep too much,
we go crazy. If we don't weep, we go crazy.

Crazy, he calls me. What a great line.
Willie Nelson looks like tobacco spit in snow.

But what a great line. Crazy, who calls me crazy?
The one I want hollers for me, STELLA

STELLA walking the floors, diva in the making,
clicking my Italian boots' steel-edged heels.

Vagina or Vocation. Vaginal, vocational
Love or Lust or Limits at the gas station.

Everything reckons on days when heaven releases perfume.
Come claim my loving heart, I call to him.

I want you funny and hungry
and wrinkled with sweat.

Sunday morning, after Church
the Village sparkles. I tell a good friend.
You know, *I can smell men.*

➤ FOR SUSAN WHEELER

New Year

One more year alive.
Exploding fireworks precisely timed.
At the corner of the avenue young men slapped five.
Discrete are the rhythms of waltzes
and rap/funky on the side of strong arm
around slender waist. Big skirts, big hair

big to-do as plastic champagne glasses bounce.
We are flourishing in the New World.

In slavery time Marilyn tells me they locked up the churches
until the rooster crowed morning and all the prayers
had been made. People on their knees know how to get up.

Praying for the one chance to rip out across the American Paradise
seeking a charged star pointing away from here.

A century or so later in Brooklyn, church folk honor
that motion north. Constellations, footprints. Those tufts of fur
caught in branches of trees, rhythms altered for the shuffle,
the crawl, the dash across thresholds:
field hand or free woman; concubine or son of liberty.

Time at the border waiting at the railway station.
Church as safe house, way station. Sanctuary.
Time at the corner. Time on the skin slapping five.

A sentimental riot endures as an old Scottish drinking song
stings the frigid air. What are these tears and that sad road ahead?

This is about liberty. About the road taken. About the shape of folk tales,
rituals, and the jailhouse door. A bottle smashed is just glass.

What the choir lacks in harmony is made up in memory.
A people made to live like beasts of burden gratefully sing of the death,
the ugly, painful, torturous death of their masters.

An innocent fiction is revealed as sirens scatter clinging celebrants
        drunken at the corner,
unsteady before their entrance to the underground just outside
        the locked church's doors
where all within pray in honor of one more year alive.
.

Meanwhile, the New Year's babies get their pictures taken.
Live at 12:01. Mothers and infants doing fine.

➤ FOR MARILYN NANCE

Saltimbanque

⯈ THAT THERE IS A PLACE OF ART IN THE CITY AND SOCIETY, THE SPACE ALLOWED TO ART, ITS DIFFERENT GUISES AND ITS VERY DIFFERENT PUBLICS, ITS PERVERSIONS IN THE COURTS AND ITS SUPPRESSION IN THE STREETS.
T. J. CLARKE, THE ABSOLUTE BOURGEOIS:
ARTISTS AND POLITICS IN FRANCE 1848-1851

1.

Suppose Daumier had behaved differently? His walks across
Paris uneventful. News banal—barricades, congresses,
the secret societies ineffectual. What would his cartoons reveal?
The fat bellied bourgeois slimmer? The masses
stepping into well made shoes?
Or would he have— as he did in private— made more paintings
of the *saltimbanques*: street performers suppressed,
by order of the State?

Were their songs too political, pornographic?
Had their children not received instruction from the priests?
Were their dancing dogs and wily monkeys better off
burned?

Have we not enough water?
Is there not enough air?

2.

Banners dirty and torn, fragmented song singes air.
Why are the revolutions of 1848 present?
Weapons in the hands of peasants, slave rebellions
in the American South, the monarchy in crisis,
plutocrats measure their new-found power in gilt, silk, velocity.

Pamphleteers for the right hand and the left.
Militarists, Marx, and monopoly capitalists,
the modern world embryonic.

3.

What a blaze was to be made in less than one hundred years.
Sorting through shadows, airborne war machines
disrupt, destroy with electrical ease.
An eleven year old's voice is suddenly burdened
with dust,
human dust as ovens roar a clinical heat.
(Attendants weep as a passage from Wagner rises
from a well-tended Victrola.)
Displaced, disloved, dissolved almost,
a patch of khaki becomes a small girl's dress,
old shoelaces are ribbons for her hair.
A population of zombies beg for cigarettes and curse.

4.

On a Saigon street, in the midday heat
or so it seems in the black and white film
a Buddhist monk in a moment
of amazing rage and pure tenderness
doused his saffron robes.
We do not see this vivid yellow.
We taste dust. Human dust.

Sous les paves, la plage.
Under the pavement, the beach.

5.

Sous les paves, la plage
Songs of freedom scorch parched throats.

Workers and students defy enforced alienation.
Rise together, spray police with pamphlets, curses,
on the very paving stones that once were danced upon
by the *saltimbanques,* their children and trained beasts.
While an ocean away, under an image of the ever defiant Che,
intellectuals, idealists, the disaffected rallied across
a hemisphere. In the mountains of Central America,
poets purged themselves in clear, cold streams,
debated desire, and learned to shoot.
Sous les paves, la plage.

6.

On a road to Biafra, in the slums of Manilla,
on the back streets of Kingston, inside the chain-linked lawns
of South Los Angeles, people make a song, new song, riot song
as a stockpile of promises collapses the shanty towns,
miners' camps, the migrant workers' buses traveling north
from Florida seats sticky with overripe oranges.

Under the pavement, the beach.
Under a stockpile of rotting promises, human stench
Bodies gunned down in daylight in Manila, Mexico City,
Memphis, Tennessee. Cameras chasing children
grabbing a solid taste of fire.

And earlier that year, Soviet tanks pressed against
the Prague Spring, a winter storm drowning flowers.

7.

Martin King sat bleeding in a Birmingham jail. He worked
his mind along the sacred stations of the cross and found,
if not solace, then the tattered cloth called dignity,
as he prayed for the souls of his jailers.

Tracing Alabama dust, his cross just heavy enough to bear,
Word could have been miracle, joy, power.
It was likely to have been song, people, or alone.
He made, in private, a face mimicking the fat, snuff-dipping guards.
Clown face turned towards jail-floor dust.
His tears roll away holy laughter. *Saltimbanque*
in a moment of amazing tenderness and pure rage.

Under the paving stones, the beach.

➣ WITH THANKS TO NATHALIE SCHMIDT FOR THE FRENCH PHRASES CREATED BY
THE SITUATIONISTS FOR THE 1968 STUDENT PROTESTS IN PARIS

ll Saints Day

Diamanda Galas screams sings
rage upon love
as winter forms
drop by cooling drop.

And earlier in that year, spring in the Blue Ridge—
pastures and hills bejeweled
with violets, dogwoods, the Judas Tree—
softens the bitter taste
of recipes for worming, for worry,
for the death of masters, overseers,
the uniformed patriarchs of a history
astonished by defeat. The burned mansions and
moth-ridden grief come back to haunt lanes
to the left and right, a clear divide

between the Black side and the white.
On All Saints Day, a wind resurrected
as dervish, spiraling dry, sharp leaves

righteous fuel for bonfires.
Honorable music to comfort the dead.

Connecticut Shore/Long Island Sound, July 4, 1998

Sunset.
We are drinking delicious beers in the pleasurable heat of this July.
Morning doves coo and a bird we cannot name
sits placidly on the telephone wire. When John talks to clients, they ask
are you living in Paradise?

What if this is the American Paradise?
The Connecticut Sound where horseshoe crabs leave
amber colored shells on the shore
as sand, rock, shells crack and spark
beneath bare feet. Children are splashing each other.
Laughter travels through the water
like lightning.
The sky opens wider and wider— lens of a large, magical camera.

When you see the purebred beagle's tail curl
against this sky, liberty glitters, the prize
worth fighting for which is why
they burn old wood on a tiny island off Indian Cove.
A giant fire cracks sunset's edge as sparklers
shimmer on the shore. Drunk are we on ice cream,
grilled meats, beer, the heat. But in brief memory, warships
bob and weave on the crystalline water.
An enemy was fought here and the patriots' fear is best forgotten.

As we, satisfied at the end of a splendid day, slip further away
from the remembrance of sacrifice, bravery, the verities of scribblers

intent on revolution even as the slave ships gorged with cargo
and rum flowed north from Barbados to New England, a trade marking
a modern genesis of a hell on earth.

Twenty-two years since the Bicentennial, our American faces register
        innocent cheer
as if knowledge was indeed the only serpent in the garden.
All the snakes were driven away from here by saints, fools and movie stars.

Late evening.
Between libido, fashion, hair style and color, class warfare
rages on the dance floor in Madison.
The only other Black face in the room seems weary of drunken disregard.
Musicians wear polished shoes or thrift store neckties.
The barmaid is Irish and tired of hassle.
And everyone watches for the first signs of cowardice, retreat.

Woe begone!
Back in van, as we rock on home, our bodies sag
beneath the weight of all these good times with the newly lucrative.
Fearful of their neighbors' flower gardens and dogs, new money hides inside
houses too vast for their high-priced half-acre lots.
Our modesty intact, we joke about tacky taste and sham security.

We are in this for long haul.
Stars pattern the darkness.
Post midnight fireworks splurge and splatter the shoreline
casting off contrails of soft color. A second twilight.

America is so young.

➤ For Maureen Owen and John Davis

My Matthew Shepard Poem

My students are rightfully spooked
someone their age was left to perish
because he preferred the company of men

My mother tells me of seeing a man lynched
back in the 30's, in Arkansas, not far from where
I grew up and grew away in the 60's.

What I know about America is that hatred
crawls through the culture like the cracks
in the San Andreas fault.

Edifices are built to withstand the inevitable
quakes, but the quakes grow stronger..
What ever we dream harmony or a reasonable tolerance
is destroyed in the wake

of men drinking and killing. Their blood lusted
laughter howling through the night.

A Black man in Texas. A white man in Wyoming.
A doctor at his window about to eat dinner with his family.
A nurse on her way to work at a clinic.

The playing field is not level. In fact, there is no playing field.
There are men enraged by change. And women bitter about it.
And people, say
gay, Black, Latino, Chinese, Japanese, Arab, or Jewish
to blame, always to blame.

The ugly men in their same wool suits and striped ties
gibber political correctness, freedom, fairness
and fuck you

every time they claim that these are acts of individuals, not of society.
Each act alone represents

singular aberrant behavior, like murder.
I can hear them say, I mean they actually lynched that boy,
even as they call this one faggot and that one nigger.
And they really, really want women
compliant and girlish
or sexless and mothering.

And if this seems like male bashing, so be it.
If the dress shoe fits, may it pinch like hell.

California Real

An airplane, nose first just
this side of the tarmac—pilot okay
police and military men walkie talkie

We slowly drive by.
Jim opens his glove compartment
picks up his camera
click, an image
and we are off towards Sacramento.

Andrew, Andy, and Jim tell flying stories
Andy's is the best. It's about being tricked into taking off.

I think we are all tricked into believing in fate,
fortune or that bad turn,
sky to earth—which plane lands on solid ground,
which one blasts water.

As if the sea's fierce equality
those who fall, die
could be neutralized by platitudes and parables.
It does not work.

I left New York City, sad at death's latest celebrity prey,
the handsome son of the slain President, his beautiful wife, her sister.
And then, the parade of clichés by men and women
well paid to say them over and over again.

What we know is that we live in an age where goodness
surprises. Where glamours—the true tricks of the trade—
are as rare as Elizabeth Taylor's violet eyes.

And even with money and media, gloss and fragrance
good character still matters, even as its shape diminishes.

A grinning cow jumping over the moon, paint peeling
as its nose dives across the cosmos,
one more wonder in a place of wonders. As if anyone
could find California real.

Part Three

aura

The most beautiful woman in the room nailed to a wall.

Her prim confidante laments the death of goddesses.
His is a feline recollection—the sibilant sound of her voice,
the droop of her eyelids; the dynamic wave of her manicured hands.

Angled brim snaps our attention. The detective listens
as if to Hermaphrodite half in shadow; half in light.
His eyes penetrate the hazy bitterness, cognac and whiskey neat.

He rattles his whisky and ice.
If only her skin were to flame
and her pulse to fall and rise again.

The most beautiful woman in the room nailed to a wall

Men's spent voices oscillate room to room.
In her house.

 # Red River

How different she is. The woman played by Joanne Dru
is neither virgin or whore. Sure, she's been around
and she knows men the way she knows this star map
that got her somewhere west of Jesus.

She's pretty, but Montgomery Clift is prettier
and knows how to control his steed.

John Wayne, our star, plays that Great American Character
the wealthy obsessive. Enraged and fixated, he will do
what he wants to do. Which is kill his son.

Wayne's performance is truly terrifying.
He is a Stetson wearing Saturn preparing to feast on Clift's
tight ass.
Could this have killed the Western?

The plot makes little sense. A race to cross Red River.
Wayne's comrades try to keep him from doing what he think he has to do,
which is kill his son.
There's cattle, dust, and a lot of scrawny men on horseback.
There are mix-ups, gunplay, and a trail to stay on or leave behind.

There's Joanne Dru disturbing this male rupture.
She's tired of moving. She's tired of unmet promises,
dead husbands, fathers, brothers, cousins. Men who lack mercy.

And unlike a host of her sisters in saddle operas,
she stops the action. Ends the feud.
Kisses the hero,
if you want to call him that, and gets her own home.

And yes, they crossed Red River.

How to Marry a Millionaire

There are three girls, always, three.
They learn to perform pratfalls
without breaking strings of perfectly matched pearls.

Two honor the cardinals—no wealthy man is out of the loop.
Just because he wears baggy pants
and his beard is untrimmed does not mean he's a bad comic.

Learn the language of tailors, bookmakers, and philanthropists.
Give the guy a chance to get used to your
hint of glamour and terrific work ethic.
Skirts tight, legs long, if possible or via bottle, be blonde.
Forget mystery, we're talking American men.

One of them cares a little less for this hunt.
She questions her companions' faith in the economics of marriage.
Who will marry a poor man, a guy who is smart, funny,
and wears his working clothes with ease?
Would she?!

But this is a comedy. No one is as they seem.
The natural-peroxided blonde wears glasses and understands
            quantum mechanics.
The older, brazen woman is not nearly as needy as she sings.
And the cynic needs the least makeup.

When rivals trip, our heroines scramble after portfolios
flung across highly polished parquet floors
deftly perform their pratfalls and break eyeglasses.

Everyone runs in and out of enormous doors
leading to or away from bedrooms.

As prey, the soon to be grooms remain unaware of their fiancées'
stealth success.
Spines stiffen.
Heart muscles contract; expand.
Lawyers caution pre nuptial.

But he is the prize for the woman who carefully places love
in its market perspective

Whispering low in front of an overly lit makeup mirror,
she reminds herself that it is just as easy to love a rich man as a poor one.
And darn it (this was the fifties), she works for her living.
Sniff. The pratfalls work.
As does the fierce rivalry among these women.
They each get the man they deserve.

The illusion of true love
frames the final reel.
In a flower filled Anglican chapel somewhere off Madison Avenue
everyone smiles as the bride in bouffant white
and the groom in a hurry to get on with it cutaway,
whisper their proper vows,
treacly music swoons as the camera portrays in close-up.

The perfect couple as they bare their strong, huge Hollywood teeth.
Avaricious carnivores, grand, swift, bountiful
Ready to kiss.

Cat on a Hot Tin Roof or Liz in Lingerie

In the era when air conditioning was placed only in movie theaters
and hospitals, the house set is filled with fans.
Big overhead whirling casting light and shadow in equal parts.
Atmospheric. Southern nobility in a last romance.
Sweat, swoon, the clinking of ice cubes in well-cut crystal.
New money and good lighting. And if lucky, the movie fills up with
Elizabeth Taylor dressed in slips and bras
with masses of black hair piled high on her regal head.

Sleek as a panther
Violet eyes and red lipstick.
The bathing beauty apotheosis.

Cat on a Hot Tin Roof in light and shadow.
Light fills out the big house where Big Daddy growls,
another kind of cat. He's in pain.

The camera pans a well-appointed bedroom
where a very healthy looking Paul Newman
tries to look drunk and crippled
by some accident of bad writing. He's in pain.

And then there is Liz in shimmering bra and slip.
She looks as if she stepped out a magazine advertisement
"I dreamed I launched a thousand jerk offs in my . . ."
Oh what a dame! She strokes, screams and purrs.
Everyone's a cat in this movie.

At first this seems to be about S. E. X.
whenever Liz and Paul mark each other's
considerable scenic territory
but then Big Daddy roars and it's about C A. N. C. E. R.

Out of nowhere arrives the pregnant sister in law
and many well-dressed, unappealing children who occasion
snide remarks from the desperate Maggie,
the writing gets better.

All these feline creatures with their shining surface beauty
are licking themselves in anticipation of some greater reward
the Big House, the Big Life but first they have to get past the Big Lie.

So there is Liz at her loveliest stroking the reluctant Brick.
He's got his bottle and his crutch and his memories of some poor schmuck
who died young (in his arms?) .
So much guilt, so little time.

Poor Brick, whose screen name anticipates a multitude
            of male nom de soap operas
will succumb to the magnificent Maggie before the final scene.

Maggie wants her baby and money and a better decorator
for this House of Pain.
Meanwhile, Jack Carson gives the performance of his career,
but no one notices because Liz wears clinging lingerie.

As if spectral, Black servants come and go
see all, know all, stash the good china and the heavy silver.
They'll cash in their patience and their secrets and move north.

They will buy property in Kansas or Wisconsin
and enjoy long stretches of storm and snow.

Hud

If a starched white shirt clings to his broad wet chest
and deer and antelope play,
it must be Texas.
Dust, highways and diners serving
very bad coffee.

Look at those teasing eyes.
Smell the smoke's slow curl
into bright sun,
Can this tale be told today?

Where else can a man be a jerk
and still make a woman's heart ache?

We want more.
More of his cool, patrician inspection
of the very core of our lusting selves.

Oh for a day to be Patricia Neal
warming up her whiskey voice
just so she can tell Paul Newman
where to go and how fast to get there.

Just watch the sun fall behind the horizon
casting out the will of God and urging the rise
of demons: drugs, dollars,

the fleeting power of men in uniform
come to kick ass,
and drag the beautiful, the mild, the musical
across piney wood floors
of tract houses and suburban drawl.

The South on the verge of existentialism.
With evil enough to require regret and redemption.
God in a thousand carry-ons
In film reels to come.

For now the jerk stands bare chested
literate, tasty.
Shading those teasing eyes.

April 1994—Two Deaths, Two Wakes, Two Open Caskets: Ron Vawter

I would have had quite a time reviewing your wake.
It was entertaining, dramatically planned.
Flowers, white flowers in vases, pots, everywhere the eye could rest—
the anteroom perfumed by blooming whiteness.
Flowers for a man full of mad love for his generation's masculine beauty,
militantly muscled then shrunk down slow.
You were laid out in your "Roy Cohen" costume, that jacket's
        deep velvet plushness
contrasting with the stiff whiteness of the satin tufts of the casket's lining.
You wore "Roy Cohen" makeup which made you look older,
the age you would have liked to reach.
Had you not had AIDS, had your heart not stopped in
        a beautiful place in Italy.
"Too soon. Too soon."

You knew the seriousness of The Joke.
 Pratfalls, you could do.
But what was better was the right gesture
 the swinging penis dance in *Frank Dell*,
 that loopy voice in *Three Sisters*;
the prim and proper lecturer in *Route 1 and 9*.
Who could fault such fault free performances?
Critics and enemies alike enjoyed your quest
for that moment when the joke worked,
the gesture transformed the actor.

The audience let go of theory.
And swooned or laughed.

In one of the miserable years I lived in Boston
The Wooster Group brought downtown Manhattan to Cambridge.
At the Captain's Bar in a downtown Sheraton, you were outrageously
flirting as you were want to do with all God's creatures.

Your voice a deep, untroubled instrument soaked gently in bourbon
or was it one of those sweet liqueurs that made everyone else's tongue shriek.
You dared me to try a dry, dry martini. And of course, I did.
And dare again, you twinkled, try two.
And we talked about what? Poetry, theater, Reagan/Bush, an era of
foul weather and Wall Street Wizards.
You were as handsome as the guy in the IBM print ad,
but then, you were the guy in the IBM print ad.
There was so much laughter.

Friends at the barricades or on bar stools.
Charmed by that twinkle. I wish I could do this memory better.
It was not that long ago.
Not that many days between a winter in Boston (brutal)
and a Spring in Manhattan (lovely, sweet) where one friends death
left me scattered some what—a story here, a color there.

Greg and you hosting a liquid Christmas party on Bleeker Street.
Somewhat frantic and cheerful as if awash part brandy/part beer.
You dressed like a thirties movie star:
George Brent, you were doing George Brent.
Stylish, suave. Cocktails at the ready,
you were happy with new work.

Pleased to have Gary Indiana set a piece about Roy Cohen for you,
just for you.
You showed us this green velvet tuxedo, a green almost black.
The plush velvet fabric camouflaged the jackets severe tailoring.
A perfect costume. Elegant, yet just the hint of the *parvenu,*
Roy Cohen on the bias.

There was laughter, an urgent kind of laughter.
Some presentiment—warriors in the desert,
the death of friends. The coarse understanding of death
too soon. Too young. Too soon.

But that laughter, it kept rising near the Christmas tree,
by the refrigerator, just outside the door.
Peace. There was no peace.

For what it's worth, you are the only actor to have made me weep.
It was a moment in *Jack Smith* where Smith pushes back the elaborate
fake Arab headgear, mascara smearing so slowly that decades fade away,
having exhaled an aria on the greatness of Lola Montes, there was a stop
from exhaustion, anger, distraction, what?
Jack Smith's seven veils parted and swayed as if in a silly dream
and you leaned away from us, transfixed by a spotlight
or an insect. How tawdry, Ron,
And oh, so very beautiful.

Part Four

April 1994—Two Deaths, Two Wakes, Two Open Caskets: Lynda Hull

Last time I saw Lynda she was pleased with the world.
We were gossiping, giggling, giving bad advice
to Michael ever in search of the perfect mate.
"You're looking in all the wrong places," we chorused
as if we could divine for him the perfect man.

As we promenaded the SoHo side streets, Lynda's cane
became a syncopating accessory. Tapping this little dance
of a body in recovery—a year of rehabilitation
after the Chicago taxi avoiding ice, instead hit her.

We are searching for the perfect black silk slip
"to make me decent," said Madam Lynda as we plowed
rows of silken wares in a store on West Broadway.
"Look at these prices!"
"Must be the store where rich guys buy presents
for their mistresses," she stage whispered.

The store manager was not pleased.
We huffily leave.
Start laughing as soon as the heavy glass door closes.

By now we are in full cry, the sun and scent of late autumn air,
electrically charged by the sybaritic
fashions flashing by, Manhattan, weekday
vacating routine, vexing Michael with girl talk.

We find the perfect black silk slip on Thompson Street
A pretty Japanese girl, so quietly chic, we mouth "princess"
is helpful, disinterested, typically shopgirl discrete.
The perfect black silk slip will slide beneath
Lynda's black beaded dress, made early in this century.

Each bead separate, sparkling hand sewn by women
in ateliers of Paris, London, Warsaw, Prague.
Women who looked like her grandmother, aunt, cousin.
Gypsy women, runaways with a keen knowledge of needle,
thread, time, ice.

It was ice, a tree, car off course, a tree
that stopped the demons, no stopped the poet,
her fugitive breath. Stopped. End of a bad winter.

The priest's homily is of a Lynda unknown to me.
A Lynda whose faith held her, transfixed in the heavy air
of this thick walled church. How had this sacred space
become familiar to her? Would her compassion, her courage,
embrace the priest's clumsy sentimentality?
Could the bells ring brighter than the string of pearls
around one of the pallbearers' neck?

Would the lilies trumpet a woman's words as dazzling
as hers spelled out, consonant and vowel on a day perfect
for picnics, lawn mowing, cleaning out the garage?

It seems that death should trouble no more the dead.
But what of a life so carefully packaged?
Which of us knew too much; others knew too little?
No word. No post card. No calls on the phone.
How last days unmasked—her drinking, her rage, trying,
trying to find some way off the chemical battlefield that had become her body.
Husband estranged. Best friends tired, perplexed. Vexed.
She seemed vexed beneath the cosmetic blush

the mortician's brush made on her thin, almost child-sized face.
Vexed. Clouds of satiny cloth enfolded her body, too small.

A column of photographs and sprays of flowers situate our sorrowful
walk from back of this square ordinary room to the open casket.

As we pass her casket, we each see:
sweet Lynda, angry Lynda,
Lynda the academician,
Lynda the magician,
sexy Lynda, fucked-up Lynda,
on the road to oblivion Lynda,
Lynda in gentle repose.

Wearing a beaded cap, her mad cap to paradise,
that one way ticket to Palookaville.
Driven through ice, feet on fire.

Femme du monde

Fat, face the color of *blanc* on *blanc*,
smelling of cheap tobacco and many unwashed garments,
from the other end of the car,
the unmistakable melody of *La vie en rose*
scratched against tender ears of Parisian commuters.
Not *La vie en rose* again, said the young Frenchman facing me.
I understood every word he said.

The old woman singing was no tiny sparrow,
no waif.
Her corpulent canine companion was equally uncouth.
She sang Piaf's signature song with a hostile gusto,
each syllable enunciated loudly.

We sniggered as the singing voice came closer.
So close we began to sing along, conspirators, smiling.
And we welcomed the doleful silence at the song's inevitable end.

I gave her a centime or was it two?
She deserved it.
Was she blind?
Did it matter?

As for me, I am weary of speaking shattered Spanish with Argentinean intellectuals
and outmoded American slang with the Moroccan grocer and his cousins
on the *Boulevard Saint Michel* near *rue Val de Grace*
And I cannot seem to count past the number, *sept!*

Gloved hands push apart the Metro's doors. It is journey's end.

I try singing Piaf's mysterious refrain, grateful for my own
soulful silly version on the walk towards the *rue Henri Barbusse,*
a short slice of street named for a revolutionary

or was he a pirate philosopher?

Tired and cheered outside my American language, I am
puzzled with the battered glamour of this city
built for electric illuminations, swift flirtations,
as I follow the paths to dead poets shaped in solemn statuary
harboring the austere lawns of the *Jardin du Luxembourg*.

Thanksgiving

There are many parched lips
as the cup of human kindness empties.
So little milk, this year

the main course consists of boiled greens (bitter)
no salt, and a tantalizing meat.
It stinks.

Fat flies link a pyramid
above rotting flesh.

On each of the round clothed tables
a bouquet of silk roses plucked
by the hands of women working in El Salvador,
Sri Lanka, the Cameroons.

What of this pain? The sharp slaps
on the knee? Sleet comes hard,
like laughter erupting a prison yard.

I will become a vegetarian!
Paradise to you, Bub.
But to me, a mystic's splendid guitar.

Jim

You looked Texas today
road hard, scrubbed brush, blown tires
gasoline islands

But later California returned—fortune's poster child
radiating. Truck full of gas,
cheap camera in the glove compartment
stuffed toys on the dashboard,
beads on the steering wheel,
a pretty girl's picture —fatherly devotion.

What is lost when love ceases
is the power to forget

the early sweetness, the late bitter
talk, the longing for renewal—we all want
Spring, but

Spring does not want us.

Persevere, the skies murmur. Persevere
you weeping poets. You funny beasts.
Hopeful and hurtful breathing dragons'

magic fire. Dry seasons last much too long
which is why deserts are vast. Floods don't help,
but days of chilly showers make for blossoms pink,
blue, violet. A soft evasion.

Drink from the lake's glacial cup. Hope for better
winters.

➣ TO JIM STORM

Female Trouble

Today, a pig veered onto the highway between New Jersey
and Manhattan and stopped traffic long enough to make Eyewitness News.

Oh Pig, pink and fat and stubborn as an angry grandmother,
standing on snow plastered ground, disregard the taunts of truck drivers,
commuter buses, drivers late for work.

That dull January day, before an operation for female trouble,
my doctor sent me to the Blood Center to give myself my own blessed blood.

Officially safe, in place of those not permitted to lay here pricked and bleeding,
the volunteer blood donors were an unexpected lot:
a biographer of Callas,
a youngish nurse who photographs only jazz musicians,
a therapist whose card I did not take, and a
Caesar's Palace head liner—slim, handsome, effusive—
who wants to be the "new Sergio Franchi." And why not?

Sergio Franchi was cool back when shark skin suits
and pointy reptilian shoes were cool
and many an Italian baritone or tenor made hearts stutter
before the Beatles let girls scream REAL REAL LOUD.

Of course, our Lady Pig has never been to Caesar's Palace.
And if she were taken there, she'd become pancetta, tasty.
Italians understand the power of bacon as well as the power of tone,

which is why the sanguine greengrocer on Ninth Avenue always gave me
an extra portion of collard greens.
"Who else eats them but we Italians and you Blacks,"
the sweet faced man told me knowing well
the ham hocks salting the iron pot's boiling liquor.

Oh let me drink with the local leather-clad rebel boys;
all movie-style glamour and cheap thrills,

who love the Pig's frenzied adventures.
At least, they will not be one of the new "Sergio Franchis."

Oh I shall praise the Pig's newsworthy chaos.
She ran amok through the suburbs of New Jersey where running amok
is not so easily done.

But hey, you never know. Pain today. Pulse.

Notes

"Days of Awe": the Days of Awe are the most solemn days of the Jewish year—the ten days between *Rosh Hashanah* and *Yom Kippur* and often coincide with the most beautiful weather that New Yorkers experience in any given year. Cynthia Kraman, to whom the poem is dedicated, is a poet and medievalist.

"*Comme des Garcons*": the name of Japanese fashion designer Rei Kawakubo's label. Her first store in New York City was on Wooster Street in SoHo.

"Sapphire": Gabriele Munter (1877-1962) was a German Expressionist painter. She was one of the first artists to exhibit with the German Expressionist group known as the Blue Rider, whose members included artists such as Franz Marc and Wassily Kandinsky with whom she had a volatile, decade-long affair.

"Comfort and Joy": dedicated to Felix Gonzalez-Torres (1957-1996), the Cuban-born, Miami-based conceptual artist who was a leading AIDs activist.

Five poems that track women's roles in American film from the 40's to the 60's:

"Laura": 1944 film noir dir. by Otto Preminger, starring Gene Tierney, Dana Andrews, and Clifton Webb.

"Red River": 1948 Western dir. by Howard Hawkes.

"How to Marry a Millionaire": 1953 film dir. by Jean Negulesco, starring Betty Grable, Lauren Bacall and Marilyn Monroe.

"Cat on the Hot Tin Roof": 1958 film adaptation of Tennessee Williams' play, dir. by Richard Brooks. Zelda Cleaver and Vince Townsend played the servants.

"Hud": 1963 film adaptation, dir. by Martin Ritt, of Larry McMurty's novel, *Horseman Pass By.*

"April 1994: Two Deaths, Two Wakes, Two Open Caskets" are linked elegies for:
—Ron Vawter (1949-1994): stage and film actor and founding member of The Wooster Group, an internationally renowned experimental theater company.

—Lynda Hull (1954-1994): poet, author of *Star Ledger* and *The Only World* (published posthumously in 1995). She was my first semester "advisor" when I started the MFA in Writing program at Vermont College. She became a friend.